A

HAIKU

SOUL

ISBN: 9780796178978

sakurabookpublishing.com

About Alta H Haffner

Alta H. Haffner is a Haiku poet whose work captures the essence of precious, fleeting moments with simplicity and depth. Born with a deep appreciation for the beauty of brevity, Alta's Haiku poems reflect her keen observation of nature and her ability to evoke emotions in just a few short lines.

Drawing her inspiration from the ever-changing seasons, the delicate balance of the natural world, and the quiet whispers of every new dawn, Alta's Haiku poems invite readers to slow down, pause, and appreciate the present moment. With a handful of syllables, she allows her readers to contemplate.

Through her Haiku poetry, Alta H. Haffner reminds us of the beauty that can be found in simplicity, the power of mindfulness, and the importance of being fully present in each moment.

Contributing Haiku Souls:

RJ Tungsten
Charles Haffner
Rajshree Nipane
Karen A Winering
Vivian Chopelas
Jacopo Rubini

A beautiful collection of Haiku, Tanka and Renga poetry by zen poets. This book is reflective and introspective. Explore the Japanese culture and language within these creative pages.

I am often asked, "Why Haiku?" and at first, years ago, all I could muster up to say was because I love it. These days, after years of learning and expanding and applying my soul, I have come to know, without a single doubt, that Haiku, as well as the traditions of Japan, lives deep inside my soul.

Sakura

Sakura~Cherry Blossom
Matcha~Green Tea
Fuji~Wisteria Flower
Hibutsu~Hidden Buddha
Nakama~Connected Souls
Awayuki~Light Snowfall
Tori~Gate to Temple

Momo-no-Sekku~
Peach Blossom Festival
Amanogawa~Milky Way
Yamayaki~Mountain Burning
Hatsuhi~first sun (New Year)
Shiogoshi~Pine Tree

through my Haiku soul
four seasons in a day lived
a life full of change

silently gazing
pensively dreaming, reflect
blossoms in full bloom

Written by
Vivian Chopelas

brought to tears of joy
she reveals infinity
with her Haiku soul

calm of new morning
scented breeze of sakura
tranquility felt

ever-changing soul
sun fire at the dawn clouds
mirror of my thoughts

Matcha

footsteps on dew green
icicles of snow melting
hot matcha steeping

dark silent night sky
owl hoot in the distant oak
restless thoughts looming

delicate pastel
dancing to the ground with wind
life changes swiftly

amber crunching leaves
winter will be over soon
soul embraced nature

silver glow river
colorful butterflies dance
poppies swaying slow

strolling through meadow
gentle hush masked the forest
trees awaiting touch of spring

banished winter chill
thin light through puffy white clouds
birds feast first candy

sand between my toes
foamy waves, footprints vanished
collecting pearl shells

Wisteria

wisteria bloom
lavender sway, lazy wind
butterfly medley

sunset silhouettes
shadows in garden of peace
bamboo scented breeze

hibutsu, Buddha
sacred temple pilgrimage
gain enlightenment

Nakama~our souls
forevermore connected
banded so closely

Awayuki~ligt snow
soft misty snow blanket fall
icy chilled winter

Momo-no-Sekku
festival of peach blossoms
pretty pink petals

ocean waves linger
darkest midnight skies above
thunder whispering

chilled blue undertone
icy breeze curling around
white sun-kissed blossoms

Amanogawa
cluster of banded bright stars
stargazing lovers

Yamayaki fire
burning old vegetation
magic spring fireworks

Hatsuhi~first sun
beginnings, forgotten old
tangerine sun glow

syllables heal souls
through a peaceful garden path
pastel sakura

a lazy full moon
wandering around the pond
autumn amber dusk

on the temple bell
await rainbow butterfly
fresh sakura breeze

dry sage leaves burning
cleansing old sin, end bad vibes
fragrant smokey air

graced by a bright moon
blazing sun in deep slumber
stars above Tori

first summer rainfall
autumn wind vanished again
chanting and dancing

dewdrops glistening
icy winter storm lurking
crow in the distance

soaking up soul words
all seventeen syllables
breathing, exhaling

soft lilac blanket
a peaceful embrace of calm
perfect harmony

Written by
RJ Tungsten

pagoda pond view
cherry blossoms reflected
mountainous backdrop

contemplate your thoughts
the heat of a summers night
a path of hope felt

dance on Sakura
a pastel pathway of hope
green tea at first dawn

Haiku, my first love
syllable by syllable
soaked in nature's gift

sacred reflecting
spiritual peace and love
unconditional

inhale Sakura
exhale syllables daily
fragrant poetic

a silent night sky
distant sound of temple bell
the stars shining bright

breathing in and out
allow slow breathing pattern
breeze rustling across

wispy clouds swaying
standing on the river's edge
an earthy ' morn breeze

a Sakura breeze
hold this dreaded pain for me
waterfall of tears

**Written by
Rajshree Nipane**

a nice day in spring
beneath the bright golden sun
buds of flowers bloom

**Written by
Charles Haffner**

stills of Sakura
beautiful colored blossoms
treasures of Japan

a calm mind within
encapsulated in peace
devine energy

ocean blue tranquility
still, without any chaos

Written by
RJ Tungsten

stifling summer heat
dissipates, falls red carpet;
leaves start to crimson

Written by
Vivian Chopelas

crowded loneliness
a rare blossom overlooked
shining among weeds

Written by
Karen A Winering

stardust lights my way
on a path that might have been
I wake up, alone

**Written by
Rajshree Nipane**

mystical moonlight
in December winter night
a magic in sight

Mii-dera found
survived more raging fires
poured sacred knowledge

butterflies flirting
a path of soft Sakura
light raindrops drizzle

Shiogoshi pine
shiny droplets of moonlight
fallen and scattered

slow waves of blossoms
a sunny day cascading
shifted direction

tiny beads of dew
caress Sakura at morn
temple bells echo

ancient temple grounds
wrapped in early morning haze
mountain and garden

whisper silently
chanting to Lotus Sutra
national treasure

Matsuo Bashō (松尾 芭蕉, 1644 –
November 28, 1694), born
Matsuo Kinsaku (松尾 金作)

Matsuo Basho lived
Iga, birthplace of master
inhale syllables

reading and learning
some saw you as poor peasant
my Haiku mentor

Written by
Vivian Chopelas
& Alta H Haffner

azure sky above
feeling safety in the blue
forever dreaming

Karen A Winering & Alta H Haffner

autumn leaves falling
interrupt my dreams of you
matcha at dawns light

Your warmth, once real to me
daydreams tingle through my soul

Rajshree Nipane & Alta H Haffner

never-ending awe
fading light of settling sun
dust clouds all around

horizon of pastel hues
still, quiet contemplation

Japanese tan Renga

Jacopo Rubini, an Italian classics professor and founder of the Latin haiku writing group Opaca Fronde & RJ Tungsten, author of the amazing Haiku book" Girasole - A Walk Through The Seasons"

Stellae hàcce nòcte
Sunt núbilā àltiòres,
Quae díscernàntur -

(Latin)

Nón visaé tamen àdsunt,
Númen tàmquam amat úsque

In the clouded night,
The stars cruising too high
To catch their sight -

Ever present yet unseen
Like God's everlasting love

Charles Haffner &
Alta H Haffner

hushing the high winds
solo traveler listens
stepping, leaves crunching

reliving past memories
autumn deepens to coral

Charles Haffner &
Alta H Haffner

moonlit mountain pass
stars over the Mogami
scenery of love

nature and our syllables
written with each passing step

a full autumn moon
resting in the darkest sky
mountains and rivers

syllables heal souls
through a peaceful garden path
pastel Sakura

on the temple bell
await Sakura
rainbow butterfly

unconditional
souls feel daily syllables
together always

footprints in the sand
ocean waves crash high and low
happy seagull greets

peace and silence evermore
a whispering wind echos

keep peace in your soul
even through chaos, be still
strive for your calmness

in a summer haze
dance to the song in your heart
thunder storm arise

soft meditation
truth between the path to soul
unfolding lotus

amber leaves falling
a path to new beginnings
breathe in the 'morn breeze

Charles Haffner &
Vivian Chopelas

Night birds serenade
empty paper beckons me
thoughts I can not find

pictures in my head, now penned
sweet past and present collide

an endless winter
a fireplace to ruminate
ancient thoughts linger

write with your soul and
imagine a world full of
Sakura blossoms

reflecting deeply
the temple bell sounds echo
time for quiet rest

moon resting among
swaying Sakura petals
chanting faintly heard

an evening mantra
allow petals to bloom and
inhale fragrant gifts

we share hurt and pain
inhale the beauty of words
heal through syllables

ocean waves splashing
the sun embracing my soul
healing and breathing

**Written by
Vivian Chopelas**

maybe stars in me
are reflections from afar
cosmic gifts of light

More books by Alta H Haffner

9 780796 178978